Put each word into the correct sentence.

respect suspicion conversation predicted
gazed intercepting incredible radio persuade

The boy .... up at the stars.

I wish I could .... my mum to buy me a bike.

She was listening to her favourite song on the ....

Two women were having a .... on the bus.

The teacher .... who would forget their homework!

He had a .... they were planning a party for him.

The opposing team kept .... the ball.

All the children had .... for the headteacher.

Their trip to the zoo had been ....!

Which words have a similar meaning to the focus word? Write them in the spaces around the word.

special

Read Part 2 of 'The Mystery of the Red Moon'. Record your thoughts about each of the three questions in the spaces below.

The looking question is ...
How did Aziz learn to build the radio?

The clue question is ...
Was Ramata impressed by Aziz?

The thinking question is ...
Will the villagers be cross with Aziz?

Do you have any questions? Write them here.

Think about the conversations you have had about this text. What more have you learned? Complete the activity below.

What do you think about Aziz now? Write as much as you can.

Circle the best words that describe Aziz.

kind clever resourceful sneaky friendly
generous honest mischievous lonely

Use your words to write a description of Aziz.

Feedback

Which words have a similar meaning to the focus word? Write them in the spaces around the word.

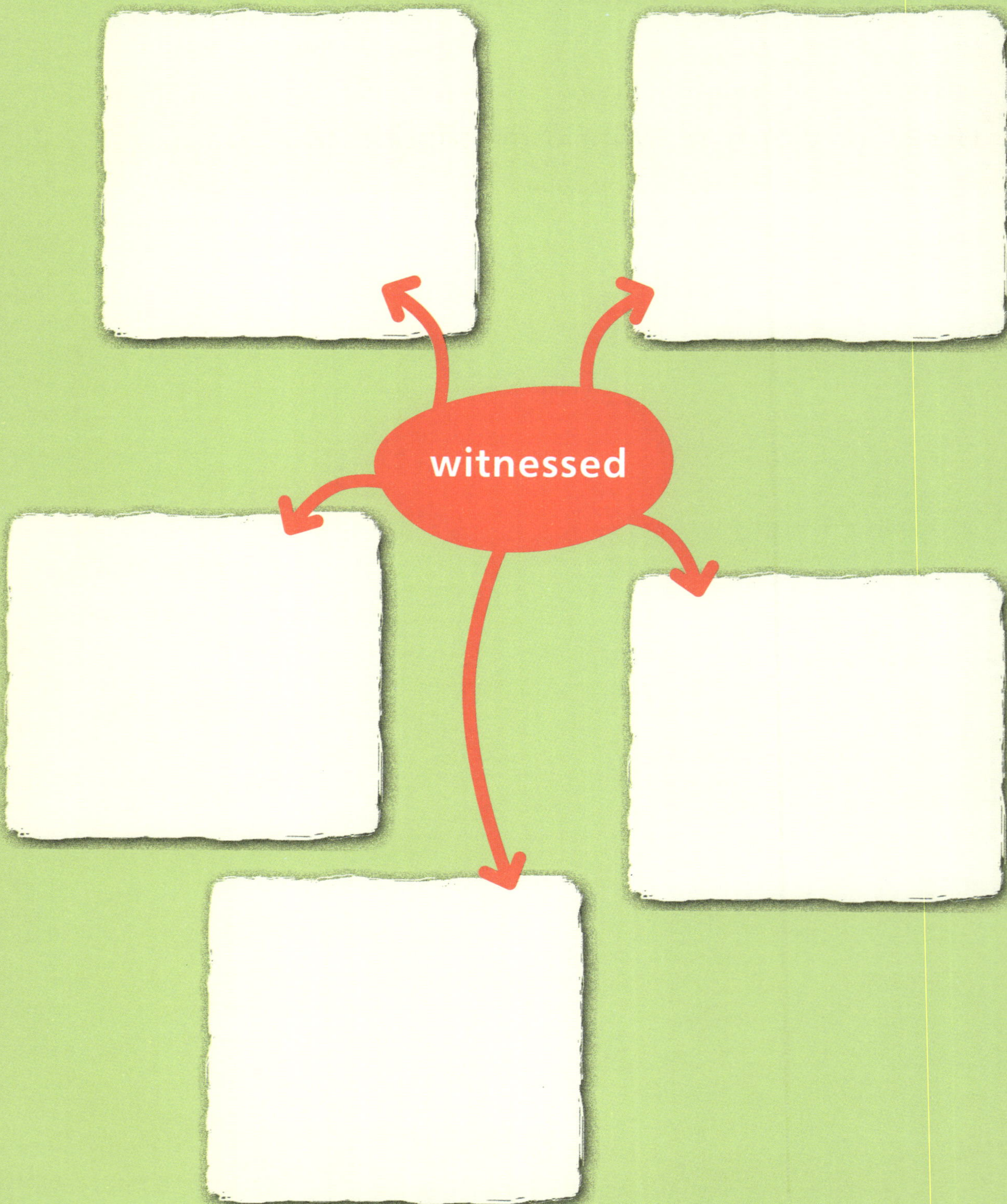

Draw lines to match the bold word in each sentence to the word or phrase which is closest in meaning. Look up any words you don't know in a dictionary.

Tomek found it difficult to **manoeuvre** his car into the tight space.

Antonio **wrestles** with his spelling homework.

Let's go out – it's a **glorious** day.

We could see Monica's **stamp** on the room: pink cushions, pink curtains and a pink duvet.

Sally ran with the ball, **dodging** the other players.

Finally, Charlie's tantrum **subsides** and he falls asleep.

wonderful

moving to avoid

cleverly move

calms down and stops

struggles

mark

Read 'Hummingbird'. Record your thoughts about each of the three questions in the spaces below.

The looking question is …
How does the hummingbird move in the storm?

The clue question is …
What does the hummingbird think and feel during the storm?

The thinking question is …
How would you feel if you were caught up in Storm Erika?

Do you have any questions? Write them here.

Think about the conversations you have had about this text. What more have you learned? Complete the activities below.

Explain what makes a hummingbird a clever flyer.

Explore how a storm is like a living thing.

Imagine you met someone from Dominica. What would you ask them?

Summarise what happened in the text you have just read using the flowchart below.

What does the hummingbird see?

It begins to rain – what does the bird do?

Storm Erika arrives – what does she do?

How does the hummingbird find food?

What does she do for the rest of the storm?

What happens after the storm?

Feedback

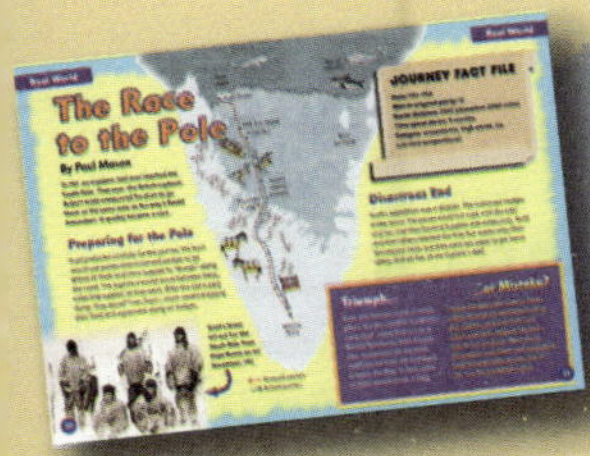

Explore the focus word by completing the activities below.

Write a definition for the focus word.

Make up a sentence using the focus word.

explorer

Write a word or phrase that means the same as the focus word.

Draw a picture of an explorer.

Do you know what the words below mean? Record your thoughts about the meanings, then look up each word in a dictionary.

I think this word means ...	The definition in the dictionary is ...
motorised	
supplies	
depot	

Read 'The Race to the Pole'. Record your thoughts about each of the three questions in the spaces below.

The looking question is ...
How did Scott and Amundsen move their supplies?

The clue question is ...
Why did Scott and Amundsen race to the Pole?

The thinking question is ...
Why do people explore dangerous places?

Do you have any questions? Write them here.

The Race to the Pole

Think about the conversations you have had about this text. What more have you learned? Complete the activities below.

Do you think Scott's expedition was a success or a failure? Explain why.

Imagine how Scott felt when he found out that Amundsen had reached the Pole first.

Describe an adventure you would like to go on.

Imagine you are interviewing Robert Scott about his trip to the South Pole. What questions would you ask? Write three questions on the clipboard below.

1

2

3

Feedback

How many words can you make from the focus word? Write as many words as you can in the space below.

For example: head, dine, lean

headlines

Change each word so that it fits in the sentences.

settle in

We .... to our rooms, then we ran outside to play.

Aisha has moved seven times and is very good at .... to a new school.

Once she ...., she'll be fine.

experience

I was very alarmed when I .... Dad's cooking for the first time.

Jim had lots of new .... on his first Scout camp.

Sally had never .... anything as scary as the Ghost Train before.

traditional

.... we have an Assembly to say goodbye to the Year 6s.

My favourite Christmas .... is opening presents!

We have been learning about the .... of other cultures.

Read 'Leaving Home'. Record your thoughts about each of the three questions in the spaces below.

The looking question is ...
How does the narrator feel before her move to England?

The clue question is ...
In the end, do you think the narrator likes living in England?

The thinking question is ...
What do you think makes a place a home?

Do you have any questions? Write them here.

Think about the conversations you have had about this text. What more have you learned? Complete the activities below.

Speculate on why people move from one country to another.

Discuss whether the narrator was lucky to have moved to England.

Describe what you need to make a home in a new country.

Summarise what happened in the text you have just read using the flowchart below. Use the headings to help you.

Newspaper

Mum, Dad, Gran

Boat

Arrives

Snow

Home

Feedback

Change each word so that it fits in the sentences.

reliable

Our car is very ....,
so let's take yours instead.

Year 6: I'm .... on you to behave!

Don't .... on me to remember – I'm likely to forget.

honours

Many towns have ....
their war heroes with memorials.

Captain Jones thought it was a great
.... to meet the Queen.

Maria Dickin believed that
.... the animals who
went to war was important.

courageous

Ravi found his .... and
ran out onto the stage.

Pat and Amy .... saved
Tom from the bullies.

Her .... was admirable.

Draw lines to match the bold word in each sentence to the word or phrase which is closest in meaning. Look up any words you don't know in a dictionary.

Chen thought he was lost but his dog's strong **homing** instinct helped him to find the way.	the main office
The boys were sent back to the park with a **mission** to find their coats.	missiles
Many companies have their **headquarters** in London.	workers on a ship
The ship had a **crew** of twenty people.	brave and determined
Soldiers wear strong helmets to help protect them from **enemy fire**.	a challenging task
The plane landed at the **airbase** late at night.	ability to navigate home
My **plucky** brother does not let anyone boss him around.	military airport

Read 'Pigeons Rule the Roost!'. Record your thoughts about each of the three questions in the spaces below.

The looking question is ...
How did Winkie save the lives of the airmen?

The clue question is ...
How can pigeons send messages secretly?

The thinking question is ...
Should animals be used in war?

Do you have any questions? Write them here.

Pigeons Rule the Roost!

The pigeon secret service

Think about the conversations you have had about this text. What more have you learned? Complete the activities below.

Argue for or against Paddy the pigeon being given a medal for his work.

Speculate on the problem of using pigeons for messages.

Justify making animals work for humans.

Give each part of the text a mark out of 10.
Write your reasons in the spaces provided.

Pages 22–23

/10

Pages 24–25

/10

Pages 26–27

/10

Feedback

Look at the pictures and the words, then look up the words in the dictionary. What do you think they mean? Write your answers in the spaces.

nerves

My Notes

husky

My Notes

reins

My Notes

Put each word into the correct sentence.

dollop clan conditions combined
daring marginally succulent lurch

The .... strength of the dogs made the sledge go fast.

When Mum wasn't looking, Ben took a second .... of ice cream.

The huge waves made the boat .... from side to side.

The Thompson .... meet for a huge picnic every August.

The highwire walker set off on his .... journey across Niagara Falls.

The hot and stuffy .... in the classroom made everyone very sleepy.

The strawberries were so sweet and ...., we ate until our fingers were red and sticky.

Urmar's handwriting is terrible and John's is only .... better.

Read Part 1 of 'Nanuck's Tale'. Record your thoughts about each of the three questions in the spaces below.

The looking question is ...
What problems does Nanuck have on the expedition?

The clue question is ...
What is the purpose of the expedition?

The thinking question is ...
Why do people want to go to the North or South Pole?

Do you have any questions? Write them here.

Think about the conversations you have had about this text. What more have you learned? Complete the activities below.

Discuss whether or not the dogs were well cared for.

Argue whether or not the dogs should have been taken to the Pole.

Speculate on the value of people travelling to the Poles.

How does Nanuck feel at the start of his adventure? Circle evidence in the text to support your answer.

No-one had warned us that the boat taking us to the start of our adventure would heave up and down. That, combined with a huge dollop of excitement and nerves at what might lie ahead, made my stomach lurch with every ocean wave.

It had all started so well. As the masters came to take us to the boat, my parents were bursting with pride. It was me, Nanuck, of the Greenland husky clan who'd been hand-picked by a world-famous explorer to take part in this daring endeavour!

Feedback

Do you know what the words below mean? Record your thoughts about the meanings, then look up each word in a dictionary.

I think this word means ...	The definition in the dictionary is ...
buffered	
crevasse	
hauled	

Use the bold words to write your own sentences in the spaces provided.

It was so **bitter** outside that the boys only played football for 20 minutes.

We walked miserably for two hours in **relentless** rain.

As Robert lay in bed, he listened to the **muffled** sounds of the television downstairs.

Tom was **sprawled** on the sofa eating pizza when his mum came home from work.

Read Part 2 of 'Nanuck's Tale'. Record your thoughts about each of the three questions in the spaces below.

The looking question is ...
How did Nanuck save a man's life?

The clue question is ...
How have Nanuck's feelings changed?

The thinking question is ...
How will Nanuck remember his time in the Arctic?

Do you have any questions? Write them here.

Think about the conversations you have had about this text. What more have you learned? Complete the activities below.

Speculate on how the man fell into the ice.

Speculate on the ways in which the adventure has changed Nanuck.

Discuss the purpose of activities that are hard but rewarding.

What do you think will happen next?
Explain your prediction in the space below.

I predict ...

Feedback

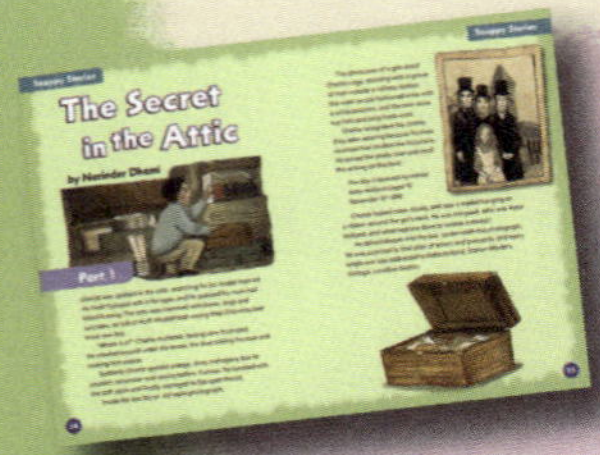

Draw lines to match the bold word in each sentence to the word or phrase which is closest in meaning. Look up any words you don't know in a dictionary.

Joshua had **crammed** so much into his bag, he couldn't do the zip up.	rummaged
The barn owl roosted in the **eaves** of the outhouse.	a dark coloured wood
The room was luxurious but old-fashioned, with a **mahogany** sideboard, velvet curtains and photographs in silver frames.	clasp
Paul had forgotten to shut the **catch** on the purse, so all the money had fallen out!	stuffed
As Deepak **fumbled** about in the dark looking for the light switch, he stubbed his toe.	under the roof
Mr Mestopholes **delved** into the bag and out came a rabbit!	felt clumsily

Use the words and phrases in the word bank to label the picture. Look up any words you do not know in a dictionary.

pinafore | top hat | frock coat
Victorians | sepia photograph

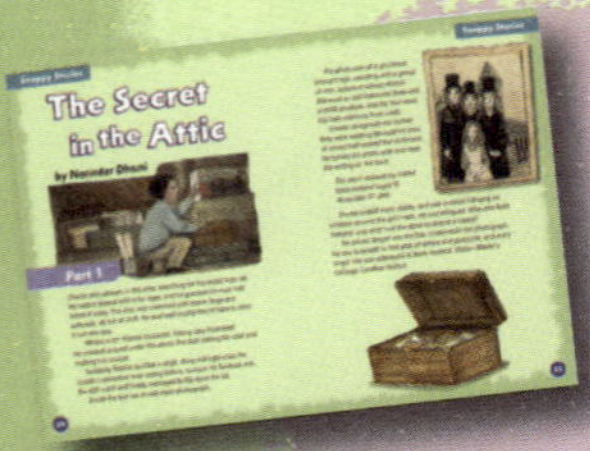

Read Part 1 of 'The Secret in the Attic'. Record your thoughts about each of the three questions in the spaces below.

The looking question is …

What is the "secret in the attic"?

The clue question is …

Why was Katie given a medal?

The thinking question is …

Why is Charlie interested in Katie's story?

Do you have any questions? Write them here.

Think about the conversations you have had about this text. What more have you learned? Complete the activities below.

Justify Charlie's actions in opening the box.

Discuss the reasons that people are given medals.

Speculate on what the other letters in the box might say.

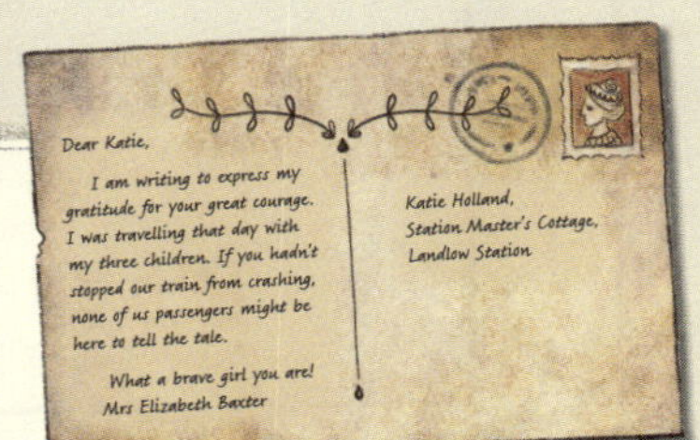

Imagine you are interviewing Katie Holland about the day she stopped the train. What questions would you ask? Write three questions on the clipboard below.

1

2

3

Feedback

Explore the focus word by completing the activities below.

Look up the focus word in the dictionary and write a definition.

Make up a sentence using the focus word.

tarnished

Draw a picture of something that is tarnished.

Explain how something might get tarnished.

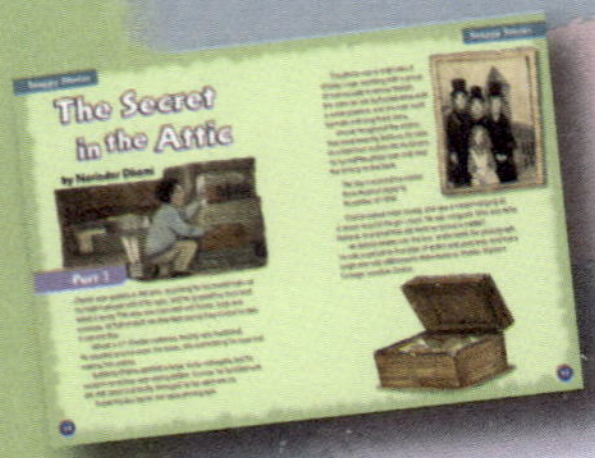

Put each word into the correct sentence.

inscription **fragile** **slammed** **blustery**
embankment **clippings** **frayed** **oak**

Every time Tony was in the newspaper, his mother cut out the article and added it to her collection of ....

Please be careful with that: it is .... and very precious to me.

It was a very .... night and the wind howled through the trees.

A mighty .... tree grows from a tiny acorn.

Rosie and Jane rolled down the grassy .... around the castle until they felt sick.

Mr Pointing .... on the brakes when he saw the dog run into the road.

The .... on the back of my granny's watch says: Daisy Lambert 20 May 1942.

The ribbons on my ballet shoes have become .... at the ends.

Read Part 2 of 'The Secret in the Attic'. Record your thoughts about each of the three questions in the spaces below.

The looking question is …

How and why does Katie stop the train?

The clue question is …

How do we know that Katie lived a long time ago?

The thinking question is …

How did being the Station Master's daughter help Katie to stop the train?

Do you have any questions? Write them here.

Think about the conversations you have had about this text. What more have you learned? Complete the activities below.

Explain what you would have done in Katie's situation.

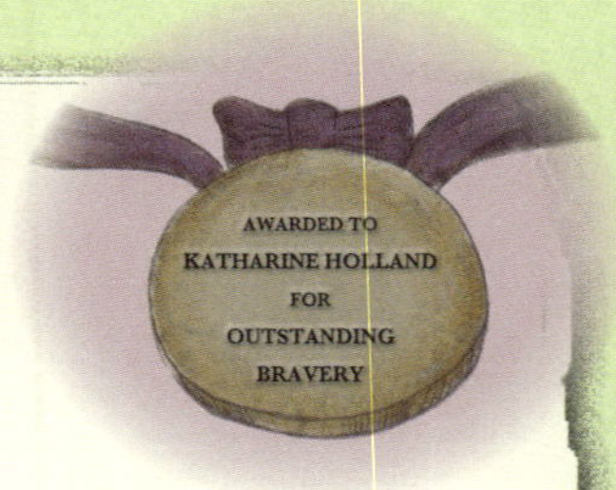

Speculate on how Katie's story would be different if it took place today.

Imagine how the events of the story might have changed Katie's life.

How do you think each character will react to Katie saving the train from crashing? Write your predictions in the spaces provided.

The Station Master

The mother on the train

Katie

Feedback

Reading Goals

This term I aim to …

Find a new author I like!

Read a play with friends!

Read the book of my favourite film!

Learn a poem by heart!

Group Discussion Rules

- We will listen carefully to the person who is speaking
- Everyone should have a chance to speak
- We will give reasons for our ideas
- We can ask others for reasons if they don't say them
- We can agree and disagree politely with each other
- We will respect each other's ideas and opinions
- We will share all the information in the group
- We will try to reach an agreement together if we can

Add any other group discussion rules your class or group has decided on here:

- ....
- ....
- ....
- ....
- ....

Reading Tracker

Book Title: ....

Author: ....

Date finished: .... Score out of 10 ☐

Book Title: ....

Author: ....

Date finished: .... Score out of 10 ☐

Book Title: ....

Author: ....

Date finished: .... Score out of 10 ☐

Book Title: ....

Author: ....

Date finished: .... Score out of 10 ☐

Book Title: ....

Author: ....

Date finished: .... Score out of 10 ☐

Book Title: ....

Author: ....

Date finished: .... Score out of 10 ☐

Book Title: ....

Author: ....

Date finished: .... Score out of 10 ☐

Book Title: ....

Author: ....

Date finished: .... Score out of 10 ☐

Book Title: ....

Author: ....

Date finished: .... Score out of 10 ☐

Book Title: ....

Author: ....

Date finished: .... Score out of 10 ☐

Read-alikes

If you liked 'The Mystery of the Red Moon', why not try ...

Sophie and the Albino Camel
by Sally Kindberg and Tracey Turner

The White Giraffe
by Lauren St John

If you liked 'Hummingbird', why not try ...

Come Into This Poem
by Tony Mitton

The RSPB Anthology of Wildlife Poetry
by various authors

If you liked 'The Race to the Pole', why not try ...

Perishing Poles (Horrible Geographies)
by Anita Ganeri

Shackleton's Journey
by William Grill

If you liked 'Leaving Home', why not try ...

Azzi In Between
by Sarah Garland

Sun Time Snow Time
by Grace Nichols

If you liked 'Pigeons Rule the Roost!', why not try ...

The Amazing Story of Adolphus Tips
by Michael Morpurgo

Who Scoops Elephant Poo?
by Margie Markarian

If you liked 'Nanuck's Tale', why not try ...

Pugs of the Frozen North
by Philip Reeve

Fleeced
by Ellie Irving

If you liked 'The Secret in the Attic', why not try ...

The Lottie Project
by Jacqueline Wilson

The Railway Children
by E. Nesbitt

The types of text I have read this term

- Funny story ☐
- Myth ☐
- Fantasy story ☐
- Joke book ☐
- Scary story ☐
- Story set in another country ☐
- Story set a long time ago ☐
- Newspaper article ☐
- Poetry book ☐
- Book of facts ☐
- Magazine ☐
- Fairy tale ☐
- Play script ☐
- Science fiction story ☐
- Picture book ☐
- Comic ☐

Something else? Write it here:

....

The best new words I have learned this term

Word	What it means
manoeuvre	move carefully

The best jokes I have read this term

How is a husky like
your nose on a cold day?

They both run!

Reading Record

Fill in these sheets for one story you have chosen yourself.

At the beginning

Title:

Author:

Why did you choose this book?

What score do you think you'll give it? /10

Who is the character you like most?

Has anything like this ever happened to you?

What questions do you have about the story?

What do you think will happen at the end?

At the end

Were your predictions right?

Is there anything that still puzzles you?

What score would you give this book? /10

Who do you think would enjoy this book?

The best facts I have read this term

Best Fact

Some aeroplanes in World War 2 carried messenger pigeons who could carry a message in an emergency.

Best Fact

Best Fact

Best Fact

Best Fact

Recommended Reads for Me

Think about someone in your group, class or family. What books would you recommend for them?

Recommended Reads for

....

A story I think they'll like:

A non-fiction book I think they'll like:

A poem I think they'll like:

An author I think they'll like:

What books have been recommended for you? Write them here.

Bug Club Comprehension is a fresh new approach that helps every child master comprehension. It uses a powerful and proven talk-based, mastery approach to help children develop a deeper understanding of texts.

Part of the Bug Club Comprehension programme, the workbooks provide:

- activities for each day of the teaching cycle
- clear, child-friendly designs that complement the accompanying texts
- formative assessment opportunities
- a 'Reading Journal' section for children to record their independent reading.

Series Consultants:
Wayne Tennent and David Reedy
Workbook and Teaching Card Authors:
Catherine Casey, Sarah Snashall and Andy Taylor

Published by Pearson Education Limited, 80 Strand, London, WC2R 0RL.

www.pearsonschools.co.uk

Designed by Bigtop
Original illustrations © Pearson Education Limited 2016
Illustrated by Chiara Fedele, Francesco Ghersina, Beidi Guo, Laura Horton and Bonnie Pang.

First published 2016

20 19 18
10 9 8 7 6

British Library Cataloguing in Publication Data
A catalogue record for this book is available from the British Library

ISBN 978 0 435 18088 1

Printed in the UK by Ashford Colour Press.

Acknowledgements
The author and publisher would like to thank the following individuals and organisations for permission to reproduce photographs:

(Key: b-bottom; c-centre; l-left; r-right; t-top)

27 PDSA, www.pdsa.org.uk: (PRTR)
29 Fotolia.com: furtseff (PRTR)
30 Alamy Images: US Air Force (PRTR). Fotolia.com: furtseff (cr/PRTR). **PDSA, www.pdsa.org.uk:** (tr/PRTR)
31 Alamy Images: Interfoto (c/PRTR). **PDSA, www.pdsa.org.uk**: (b/PRTR). **Shutterstock.com**: mountainpix (t/PRTR)
57 Shutterstock.com: Robbi (RJ)
62 Shutterstock.com: Robbi (RJ)

All other images © Pearson Education

ISBN 978-0-435-18088-1

www.pearsonschools.co.uk
enquiries@pearson.com